Executive Summary

The installed capacity of global and U.S. photovoltaic (PV) systems has soared in recent years, driven by declining PV prices and government incentives. The U.S. Department of Energy's (DOE) SunShot Initiative aims to make PV cost competitive without incentives by reducing the cost of PV-generated electricity by about 75% between 2010 and 2020.

This summary report—based on research at Lawrence Berkeley National Laboratory (LBNL) and the National Renewable Energy Laboratory (NREL)—examines progress in PV price reductions to help DOE and other PV stakeholders manage the transition to a market-driven PV industry, and to provide clarity surrounding the wide variety of potentially conflicting data available about PV system prices. It provides a high-level overview of historical, recent, and projected near-term PV pricing trends in the United States, focusing on the installed price of PV systems. More detailed analyses will be published in other reports. The following are the report's major findings:

- Reported price data for more than 150,000 installed PV systems (Section 2) show that, among systems installed in 2011, the median reported price was $6.13/W for residential and small commercial systems 10 kW capacity or less, and $4.87/W for commercial systems larger than 100 kW (Figure 1).[1] The capacity-weighted average reported for installed price of utility-scale PV systems completed in 2011 was $3.42/W. These data are a lagging indicator relative to the price of systems being installed or quoted today.

- The reported prices for systems installed in 2011 correspond closely to the results of bottom-up modeling of the overnight capital cost of PV systems quoted in the fourth quarter of 2010 (Q4 2010), which estimate an installed price of $5.90/W for 4.9-kW residential systems, $4.74/W for 217-kW commercial rooftop systems, and $3.93/W for 187.5-MW fixed-tilt utility-scale systems.[2] Owing to installation time requirements, Q4 2010 price benchmarks are the most appropriate comparison for 2011 reported price data.

- Reported installed prices of U.S. residential and commercial PV systems declined 5%–7% per year, on average, from 1998–2011, and by 11%–14% from 2010–2011, depending on system size. Preliminary data and bottom-up analysis suggest that the price reductions have continued in 2012. Specifically, bottom-up analysis for systems quoted in Q4 2011 (and installed in 2012) yields installed prices of $4.39/W for 5.1-kW residential systems, $3.43/W for 221-kW commercial rooftop systems, and $2.79/W for 191.5-MW fixed-tilt utility-scale systems, corresponding to a 25%–29% year-over-year reduction compared to Q4 2010 benchmarks.

- These figures are in line with analyst downward-trajectory projections for expected market pricing of PV systems and components in 2012, which also anticipate continuing reductions in component and system pricing beyond 2012. Analysts estimate that the global module average selling price will decline from $1.37/W in 2011 to approximately $0.74/W by 2013 and that inverter prices will also decline over this period. Analyst projections do not exist for balance of system (BOS) costs; however, the fact that PV system prices are substantially lower in Germany than in the United States, despite having similar module and inverter prices, suggests that substantial BOS cost reductions are possible for U.S. systems as well.

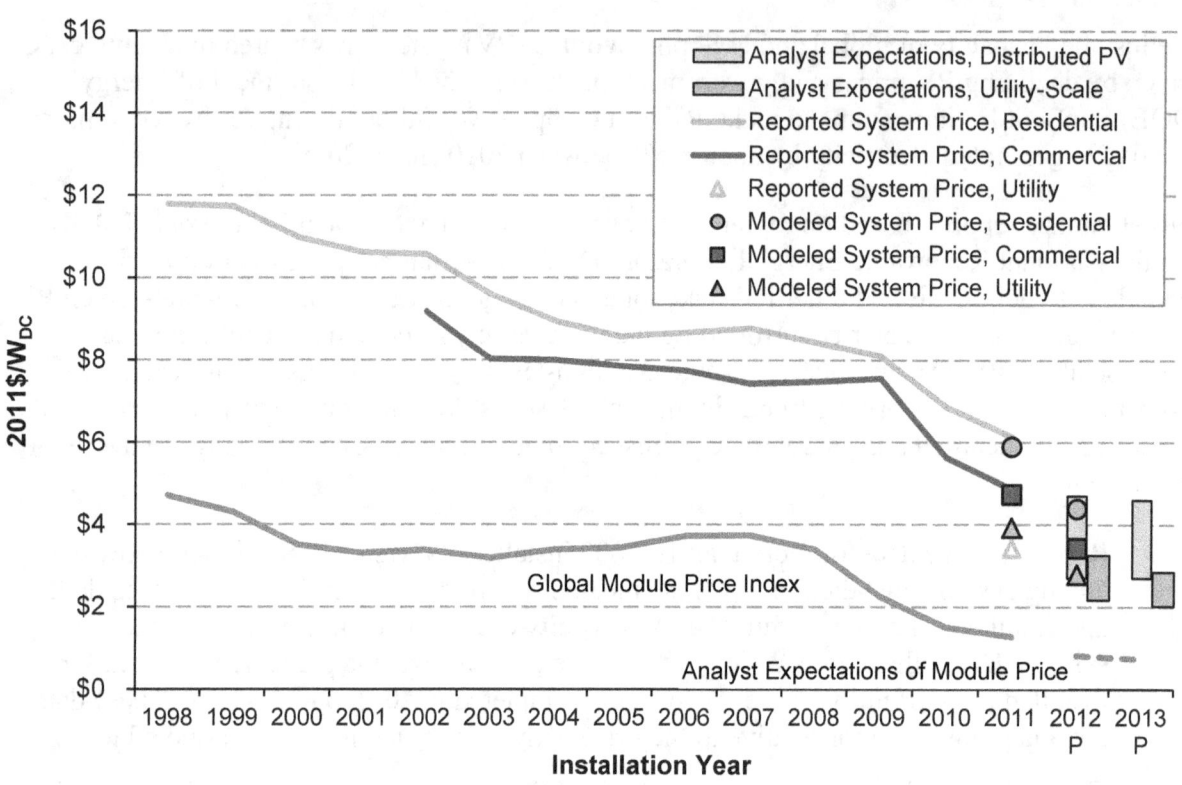

Figure 1. Reported, bottom-up, and analyst-projected average U.S. PV system price over time

Note: The reported system price for the residential market is representative of the median price reported for systems less than or equal to 10 kW in size; the median size of these systems is 5.0 kW. The modeled residential system price represents a 4.9-kW system. The reported system price for the commercial market is representative of the median price reported for systems greater than 100 kW in size; the median size of these systems is 281 kW. The modeled commercial system price represents a 217-kW rooftop system. The reported system price for the utility-scale market represents the capacity-weighted average of reported systems greater than 2 MW in size; the capacity-weighted average size of these systems is 18.3 MW. The modeled system price of utility-scale systems represents a 187.5-MW fixed-tilt ground-mounted system. Bottom-up system prices are representative of bids by an installer in the fourth quarter of the previous year. The Global Module Price Index is Navigant Consulting's module price index for large-quantity buyers.

1 Introduction

Over the past five years, annual installations of photovoltaic (PV) systems have grown 60% per year globally and 53% per year in the United States. In fact, in 2011 alone, the United States installed roughly 2 GW of the 21 GW of PV installed globally, which was a 109% increase over 2010.[3]

This rapid growth has been driven by declining PV system prices and by state and federal incentives and other forms of policy support. Many of these policies were established to stimulate PV market growth and maturity and thus spur the price reductions necessary to make PV-generated electricity cost competitive without subsidies (which are still required to make PV economic throughout most of the United States). The U.S. Department of Energy's (DOE) SunShot Initiative aims to achieve this goal by driving PV system price reductions that reduce the cost of PV-generated electricity by about 75% between 2010 and 2020.

As PV system prices continue to decline, progress must be tracked in a transparent and consistent manner so policymakers and the PV industry can manage the transition to a market-driven PV industry and so DOE can track progress toward the SunShot goals. This report helps fill this need by providing a high-level overview of past, recent, and projected near-term PV pricing trends in the United States—focusing on the *installed price* of PV systems (i.e., the upfront cost borne by the system owner in terms of dollars per watt). However, this report does not describe trends associated with PV performance, O&M costs, or other factors that affect PV's levelized cost of electricity (LCOE), although the authors recognize the critical importance of LCOE metrics.

This report draws on several ongoing research activities at Lawrence Berkeley National Laboratory (LBNL) and the National Renewable Energy Laboratory (NREL). Based on a sample of more than 150,000 U.S. PV projects, Section 2 of the report summarizes LBNL's analysis of historical and recent installed price trends for systems installed from 1998 through year end 2011 (with preliminary data for systems installed during the first half of 2012). Section 3 provides more detailed component-level benchmarks for recent PV system prices, based on NREL's detailed bottom-up engineering model of PV system costs, informed by in-depth interviews with leading installers and manufacturers. Section 4 compares the reported price data and the bottom-up benchmark price analysis methodologies and results. Finally, drawing on ongoing industry tracking activities, Section 5 summarizes near-term projections of system- and component-level pricing from various analysts and manufacturers.

This report will be supplemented by other detailed technical reports, including LBNL's *Tracking the Sun V*, which will analyze historical installed price trends extensively, and an updated version of NREL's February 2012 report on system-level installed price benchmarks (Goodrich et al. 2012).

2 Historical and Recent Reported Prices

The analysis presented in this section is derived from project-level data for actual residential, commercial, and utility-scale PV systems installed through year end 2011, with a limited set of results presented for the first half of 2012.[4] Data for residential and commercial systems are sourced primarily from state and utility PV incentive program administrators.[5] Ultimately, 42 PV incentive programs spanning 23 states provided project-level installed price data for PV systems funded through current and previous programs.[6] Data for utility sector systems were collected from diverse sources, including the Section 1603 Grant Program,[7] FERC Form 1 filings, SEC filings, company presentations, and trade press articles. Data from the same sources were also used for a limited number of large commercial PV systems not already included within the data provided by state and utility PV incentive programs.

The raw data were cleaned and standardized. Of particular note, all projects for which the reported installed price was deemed likely to represent an appraised value rather than an actual transaction price[8] were eliminated from the data sample.[9] The final, cleaned dataset consists of more than 152,000 PV systems totaling roughly 3,000 MW installed from 1998 through 2011, including 1,300 MW installed in 2011. The cleaned data sample represents approximately 76% of all grid-connected PV capacity installed in the United States through 2011 and about 69% of all U.S. capacity additions in 2011 (see Barbose et al. 2012).

As expected, the residential and commercial PV sample is dominated by California, which accounts for 62% of all systems in the dataset and 51% of systems installed in 2011.[10] New Jersey is a distant second, accounting for 8% of all systems in the dataset and 13% of those installed in 2011. Because California accounts for such a large proportion of systems in the sample (as it does within the entire population of U.S. PV systems), the national trends for residential and commercial PV described below are dominated by trends within California, which has relatively high PV prices.[11]

2.1 Residential and Commercial PV Price Trends

Figure 2 presents the median installed price of all residential and commercial projects within the sample, in each of three system size groupings, from 1998 through 2011. Among the roughly 38,000 residential and commercial PV systems in the sample installed in 2011, the median installed price was $6.13/W for systems of 10 kW or smaller, $5.62/W for systems of 10–100 kW, and $4.87/W for systems larger than 100 kW. These median values represent central tendencies; the considerable spread among the data is explored throughout the remainder of this section. As noted previously, the data for all figures in this section exclude those third-party-owned (TPO) systems for which prices reported to PV incentive programs were deemed likely to represent an appraised value rather than an actual transaction price.

As depicted in Figure 2, installed prices have declined by 5%–7% per year, on average, depending on the system size and the period over which historical data are available. Those price declines, however, have not occurred at a steady pace. Installed prices declined markedly until 2005, but then stagnated through roughly 2009, while the PV supply chain struggled to keep pace with surging worldwide demand. Since 2009, however, installed prices have fallen precipitously as upstream cost reductions—principally PV module cost reductions—worked their way through to end consumers, and as state and utility PV incentive programs continued to ramp down their incentives.

During 2010–2011, installed prices fell by $0.72/W (11%) for systems of 10 kW or smaller, $0.89/W (14%) for systems of 10–100 kW, and $0.77/W (14%) for systems larger than 100 kW. Preliminary data for the first half of 2012 (Text Box 1) show that installed prices in California have fallen further, and declines in global module prices over the first half of 2012 (see Section 5) suggest that installed system prices will continue to decline as projects in the development pipeline (whose costs reflect current module pricing) are constructed.

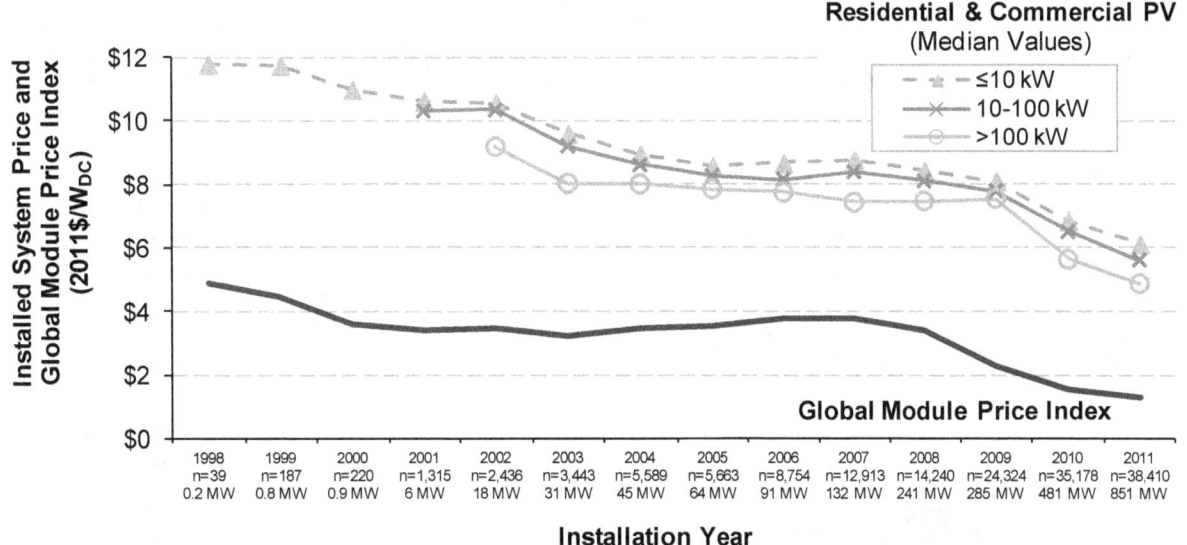

Figure 2. Installed price of residential and commercial PV systems over time

Note: Median installed prices are shown only if 15 or more observations are available for the individual size range. In addition to the installation year, the x-axis shows the number (n) of systems in the sample and the corresponding installed capacity. The Global Module Price Index is Navigant Consulting's module price index for large-quantity buyers.

Figure 2 also presents an index of global module prices over time, illustrating the close—but imperfect—historical linkages between installed system prices and PV module prices. Over the period shown, average annual module prices fell by $3.62/W in real 2011 dollars, from $4.90/W in 1998 to $1.28/W in 2011. In comparison, the total installed price of systems of 10 kW or smaller fell by $5.65/W (a further reduction of $2.03/W beyond module price changes), owing to additional reductions in non-module costs over that period. Module prices dropped by $2.52/W from 2007 to 2011. Installed system prices fell by similar amounts over this period but showed an apparent time lag behind module price reductions.[12]

The long-term decline in installed system prices is clearly the result of reductions in both module and non-module costs; however, module costs have declined at a faster pace, especially over the past several years. Thus, although module costs may have represented 50%–60% of the total system installed price several years ago, that percentage is now considerably lower. For example, if the average global module price in 2011 roughly indicates the actual underlying module costs for systems installed that year, then module costs represented just 21% of the total median installed price for systems of 10 kW or smaller. This shift in the cost structure of PV systems has heightened the emphasis within the industry and among policymakers on reducing non-module costs and, particularly, business process (or "soft") costs.[13]

Text Box 1. Preliminary Price Trends for Systems Installed in 2012: A Focus on California

Early evidence suggests that the decline in prices for systems installed in 2012 is on pace to match the decline observed in 2011. As an indication of this trend, Figure 3 compares the installed price of projects funded through the California Solar Initiative (CSI) in 2011 and the first half (H1) of 2012.

The median installed price of CSI systems installed in H1 2012 fell by roughly $0.43/W (7%) for systems of 10 kW or smaller, and by roughly $0.35/W (6%) for systems of 10–100 kW, relative to the median price of systems installed in 2011. Prices for systems larger than 100 kW, on the other hand, increased slightly during H1 2012, but that is largely due to the fact that the underlying data sample of >100 kW systems consisted of a larger share of relatively small systems in H1 2012 than in 2011 (and smaller systems tend to cost more per watt).

Within the narrower size range of 100–500 kW, the median price declined by roughly $0.18/W (3%) from 2011 to H1 2012. If CSI prices through the remainder of 2012 continue on the trajectory established during H1 2012, and if the same price reductions observed within the CSI program spread, then the national price reductions in 2012 will be similar to those witnessed in 2011. Indeed, data published by the Solar Energy Industries Association (SEIA) and Greentech Media (GTM) for the U.S. PV market show that residential and commercial PV prices in the second quarter of 2012 fell by 12% and 11%, respectively, from the last quarter of 2011.[14]

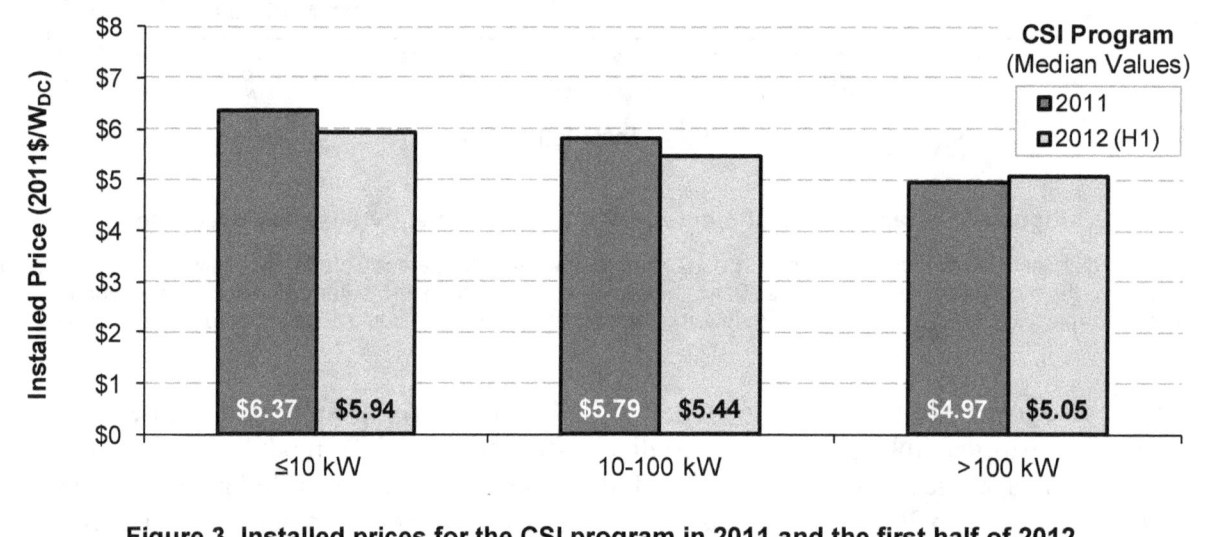

Figure 3. Installed prices for the CSI program in 2011 and the first half of 2012

Figure 4 presents the median installed price and 20th/80th percentile ranges by system size for systems installed in 2011, illustrating several key trends. First, as expected, installed prices exhibit clear economies of scale, which may be associated with price reductions on volume purchases and the ability to spread fixed costs over a larger number of installed watts for larger installations. At the two extremes (excluding utility-scale systems, which are addressed later), the median installed price was $7.69/W for systems of 2 kW or smaller versus $4.48/W for systems larger than 1,000 kW. These economies of scale are clearly strongest at the small end of the size spectrum, with the most substantial price reductions associated with increases in system size from 2 kW or smaller into the 5–10 kW range.

The second key trend illustrated in Figure 4 is the substantial variability in installed prices within any given size range, indicating regional, local, project/site-specific, and installer-specific drivers (e.g., differing degrees of experience or size). Among 5–10 kW systems, for example, the 20th and 80th percentile values span $4.98/W to $6.89/W.

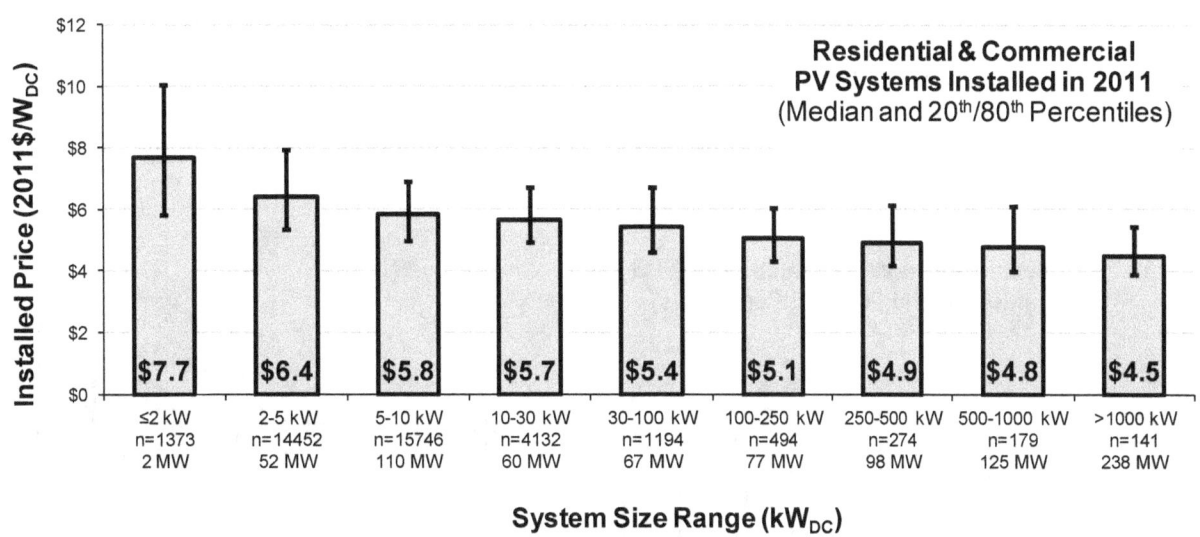

Figure 4. Variation in installed price for 2011 installations by system size

Note: In addition to the system size range, the x-axis shows the number (n) of systems in the sample and the corresponding installed capacity.

The potential importance of state or local conditions is indicated in Figure 5 and Figure 6, which compare median state-level installed prices for 2011 systems. Among systems of 10 kW or smaller (Figure 5), median installed prices range from a low of $4.9/W in Texas to a high of $7.6/W in Washington, D.C. For systems 10–100 kW in size, median installed prices range from $5.0/W in Florida and Nevada to $7.2/W in Texas (SEIA and GTM 2012). California, which dominates the overall data sample, is a relatively high cost state, which pulls installed price statistics for the entire country upward.

Differences in installed prices across states may reflect many underlying drivers. While one would expect larger or more mature state and regional PV markets to facilitate lower prices, owing to greater competition and efficiency in the delivery chain, more extensive bulk purchasing, and better access to low cost products, there is not always a strong correlation between state market size and installed system prices. Other factors also appear to be playing an important role in determining state-level pricing differences. Such factors include:

- States with less competition among installers, higher incentives, and/or higher electricity rates may have higher prices if installers are able to "value-price" their systems (i.e., charge a higher price for a system that is relatively more valuable owing to more incentives or the offset of higher-priced electricity).

- Variability in prices across states also likely derives from differences in administrative and regulatory compliance costs (e.g., incentive applications, permitting, and interconnection) as well as differences in installation labor costs.

- State-level price variation may also arise from differences in the characteristics of the systems installed in each state, such as the typical system size, roof-pitch and mounting structures, and the prevalence of tracking equipment.
- Differing sales tax treatments (some states exempt PV systems from sales tax) and sales tax rates may lead to differences in installed prices of as much as $0.40/W.[15]
- Finally, the median prices of some states shown in Figure 5 and Figure 6, especially where the sample size is small, may simply reflect idiosyncrasies of the particular systems or installers in the sample rather than any fundamental underlying state or local conditions.

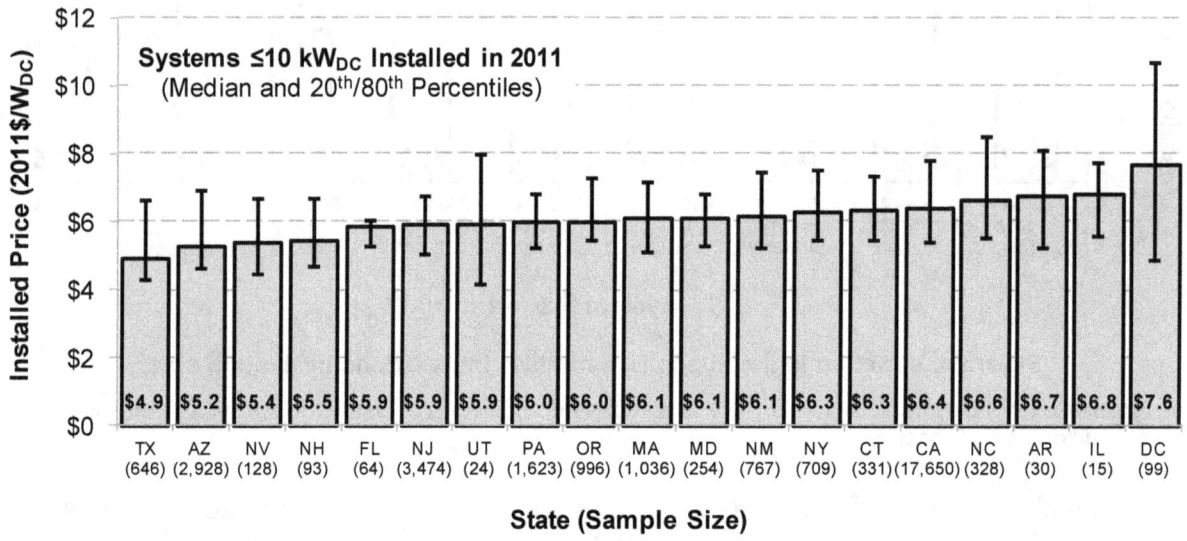

Figure 5. Installed price of 2011 residential and commercial PV systems of 10 kW or smaller by state

Note: Numbers in parentheses below each state indicate the number of observations; median installed prices are shown only if 15 or more observations are available for a given state.

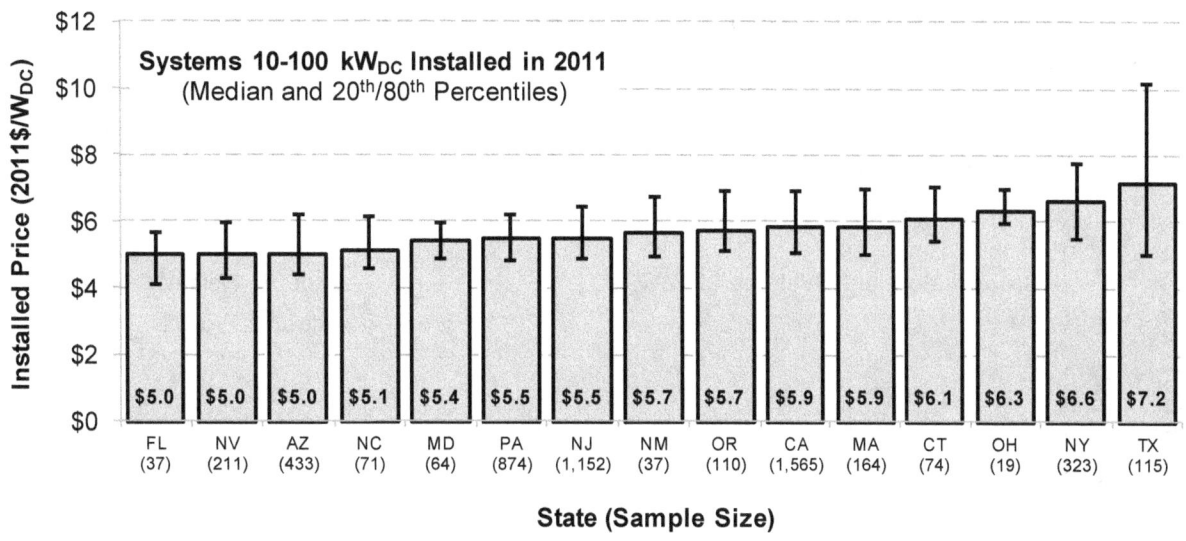

Figure 6. Installed price of 2011 residential and commercial PV systems of 10–100 kW by state

Note: Numbers in parentheses below each state indicate the number of observations; median installed prices are shown only if 15 or more observations are available for a given state.

2.2 Utility-Scale PV Price Trends

This subsection describes trends in the installed price of utility-scale PV systems, based on a more limited data sample consisting of 80 projects installed through year end 2011, totaling roughly 800 MW (~70% of all utility-scale PV installed in the United States).[16] Utility-scale PV is defined here as all ground-mounted systems at least 2 MW in size, regardless of whether the electricity is delivered to a utility or an end-use customer. There are several specific caveats to the analysis presented below, based on these data:

- *Small sample size with atypical utility PV projects.* The sample of utility-scale projects is relatively small and includes a large number of systems in the 2–10 MW size range, a small number of larger systems, and a number of larger "one-off" projects with atypical project characteristics.

- *Lag in component pricing and market conditions.* In some cases, the installed price for utility-scale PV projects may reflect component pricing and the market conditions under which power sales agreements were signed one or more years prior to project completion. The data, therefore, may not fully capture recent declines in module or other component prices or other changes in market conditions.

- *Reliability of data sources.* The installed price data for utility-scale PV projects are derived from varied sources and, in some instances, are arguably less reliable than the data presented for residential and commercial systems.

- *Focus on installed price rather than levelized cost.* Focusing on the upfront installed price ignores performance-related differences and other factors influencing the LCOE, which is ultimately the more meaningful metric for comparing utility-scale PV systems.

With these caveats, Figure 7 identifies the price of each individual utility-scale PV project in the dataset according to its year of installation. As might be expected, a wide range of prices is observed. Among projects installed in 2011, for example, installed prices range from a low of

$2.45/W to a high of $6.26/W. Discerning a time trend is challenging, given the small and diverse sample of projects. As a rough measure of this trend, the capacity-weighted average[17] installed price declined from $6.21/W for projects installed during 2004–2008 to $3.94/W for projects installed during 2009–2010, and to $3.42/W for projects installed in 2011. Clearly, however, a great degree of variability exists around those averages.

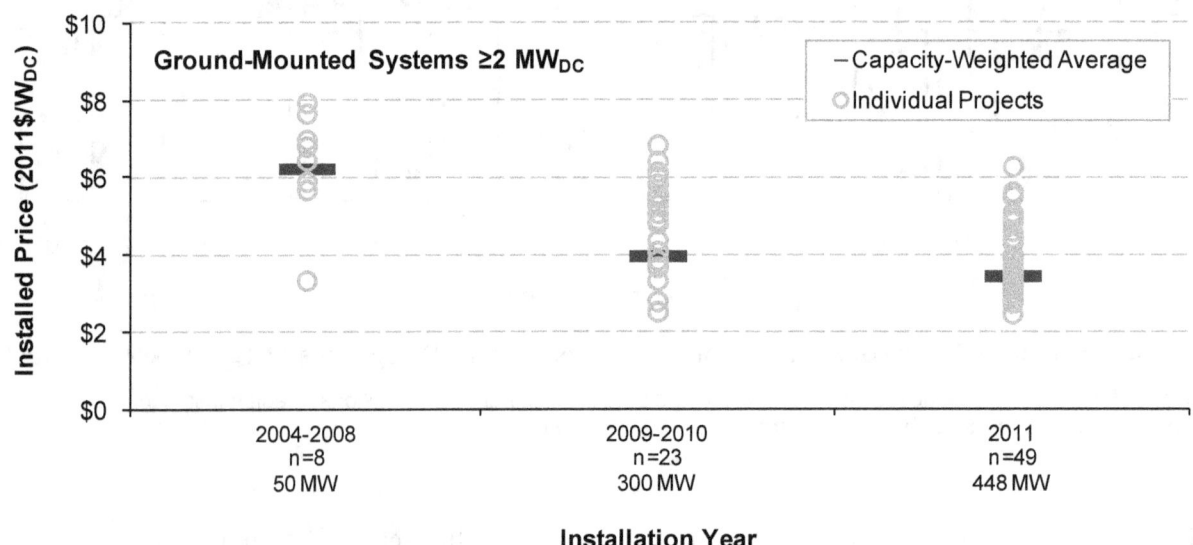

Figure 7. Installed price of utility-scale PV projects over time

Note: In addition to the installation year, the x-axis shows the number (n) of systems in the sample and the corresponding installed capacity.

The wide range of prices is partially attributable to differences in project size and configuration, as shown in Figure 8, which focuses specifically on projects completed in 2011 and distinguishes between four system configurations according to module type (crystalline silicon versus thin-film) and mounting structure (fixed-tilt versus tracking). Noticeably, the larger systems tend to have lower prices, with most projects larger than 10 MW ranging from roughly $2.80/W to $3.50/W. The projects smaller than 10 MW span a broader range, with most projects priced between $3.50/W and $5.00/W.

These project size-based trends undoubtedly reflect underlying economies of scale. However, other factors may also be at play, such as differences in the site characteristics typical of larger versus smaller utility-scale projects and differences in the characteristics of project developers (e.g., larger projects may be more likely to be developed by more experienced and/or vertically integrated companies).

The relationships between system configuration and installed price are somewhat less discernible. Among the smaller (10 MW or less) class of utility-scale projects, the thin-film projects (which include a group of five similarly configured and priced projects installed by a single southwestern utility) are all at the low end of the spectrum. Among the projects larger than 10 MW, however, no clear differences in installed prices are observable either between the crystalline and thin-film systems or between the systems with and without tracking. The absence of a visible trend does not mean that differences in system configuration have no impact on price; rather, within this small sample, the impact is lost within the myriad of other factors that influence installed prices (e.g., regulatory compliance costs for projects built on public vs. private land, whether private land is leased or owned, design requirements associated with specific climatic conditions, etc.).

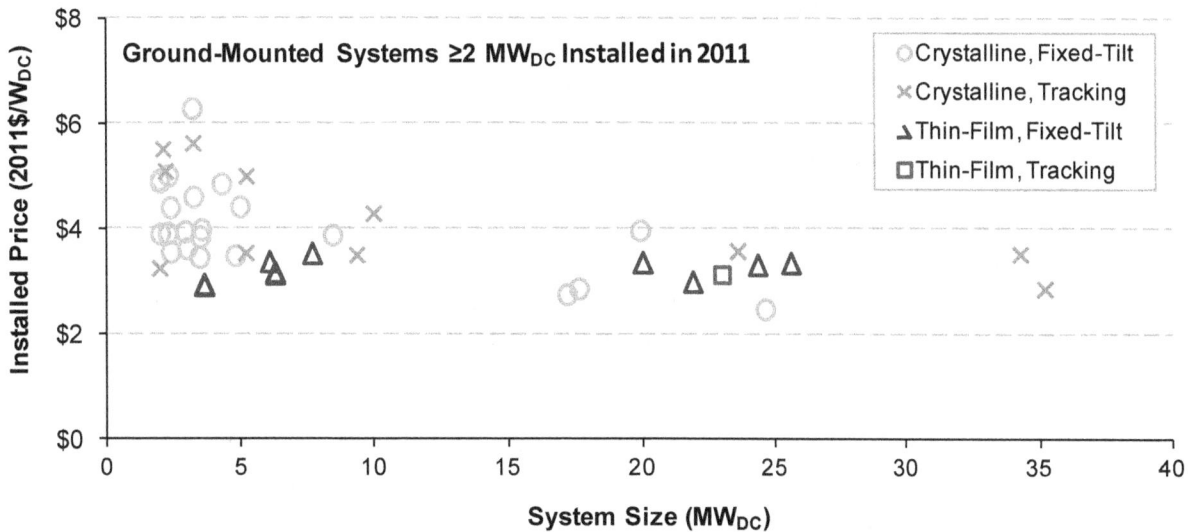

Figure 8. Installed price of 2011 utility-scale PV systems by system size and configuration

Note: The figure includes eight thin-film fixed-tilt systems of less than 10 MW; however, a number of those projects have almost identical size and installed price, and therefore cannot be visually distinguished in the figure.

3 Recent Prices from Bottom-Up Cost Analysis

In contrast to the previous section's analysis of reported PV system prices, this section summarizes a bottom-up modeling analysis of system prices (for further detail on methodology, see Goodrich et al. 2012). With this method, PV system prices are estimated by summing the costs of individual PV components and processes. Detailed cost models for specific PV system designs account for all materials, labor, overhead and profit, land acquisition and preparation costs, and regulatory costs for a PV system up to the point of grid tie-in. For example, for utility-scale PV, costs include the substation but exclude transmission infrastructure—emulating the cost estimating tools installers use to bid on projects. Each cost item is benchmarked for a given period using reported market-based costs of material and fees, national average labor rates, and conversations with industry stakeholders about actual overhead, profit, and taxes. Ultimately the data are combined to provide PV system price benchmarks—the sales price an installer would offer for a system in a given financial quarter—in the residential, commercial, and utility-scale PV markets.[18]

The goal of this bottom-up analysis is to provide an objective measure of system price under generic market conditions, free of distortions that may affect prices reported under specific site or market conditions. The bottom-up analysis complements the market data-based analysis from Section 2 because it examines in detail the individual costs underlying PV system prices. Understanding costs at this level enables the development of cost reduction roadmaps for each specific component and process, as well as the tracking of cost reduction progress for each item. At the same time, the market price analysis (Section 2) provides "ground truth" about the prices PV owners are actually paying for entire PV systems over time and how those prices vary by location, system size, and other factors—which also helps refine the bottom-up analysis.

Figure 9 summarizes the modeled benchmark prices for residential rooftop, commercial rooftop, and fixed- and one-axis utility-scale PV systems in the fourth quarter of 2010 (Q4 2010) and the fourth quarter of 2011 (Q4 2011). Costs are segmented into three categories: BOS, inverter, and module. BOS costs combine various elements including installation materials, tracking systems (if any), electrical and hardware labor, permitting and commissioning, land acquisition, site preparation, supply chain costs, installer overhead (including interest during construction and customer acquisition), profit, and sales tax.

The bottom-up benchmarked price for a typical residential system fell from $5.90/W in Q4 2010 to $4.39/W in Q4 2011, a reduction of 26%. The bottom-up commercial rooftop system price fell from $4.74/W in Q4 2010 to $3.43/W in Q4 2011, a reduction of 28%. Ground-mounted utility-scale bottom-up benchmarks also fell from Q4 2010 to Q4 2011, decreasing from $3.93/W to $2.79/W for fixed-tilt systems (a reduction of 29%), and from $4.54/W to $3.37/W for one-axis tracking systems (a reduction of 26%). BOS accounts for the majority of costs across all benchmarks, followed by module and inverter costs, respectively. Benchmarked system sizes increased between Q4 2010 and Q4 2011 due to gains in average module efficiency.

Most of the modeled cost reduction between Q4 2010 and Q4 2011 is due to the decrease in module price during that period (66% of total cost reduction for the residential benchmark was attributed to module cost reduction, 73% for commercial rooftop, and 80% for utility ground mount with fixed axes). However, BOS costs also decreased during this period because of increased module efficiencies, better supply chain management, and improved labor efficiency.

While the bottom-up modeled installed PV system prices in Figure 9 represent typical systems, several factors may cause differences in actual system prices across the country. PV system prices vary across market sectors based primarily on differences in system scale and installer channels to market (i.e., supply chain costs). Excluding differences in system size, results for any individual system may also vary based on local labor and permitting costs, technology selection decisions, installer productivity, and site-related costs.

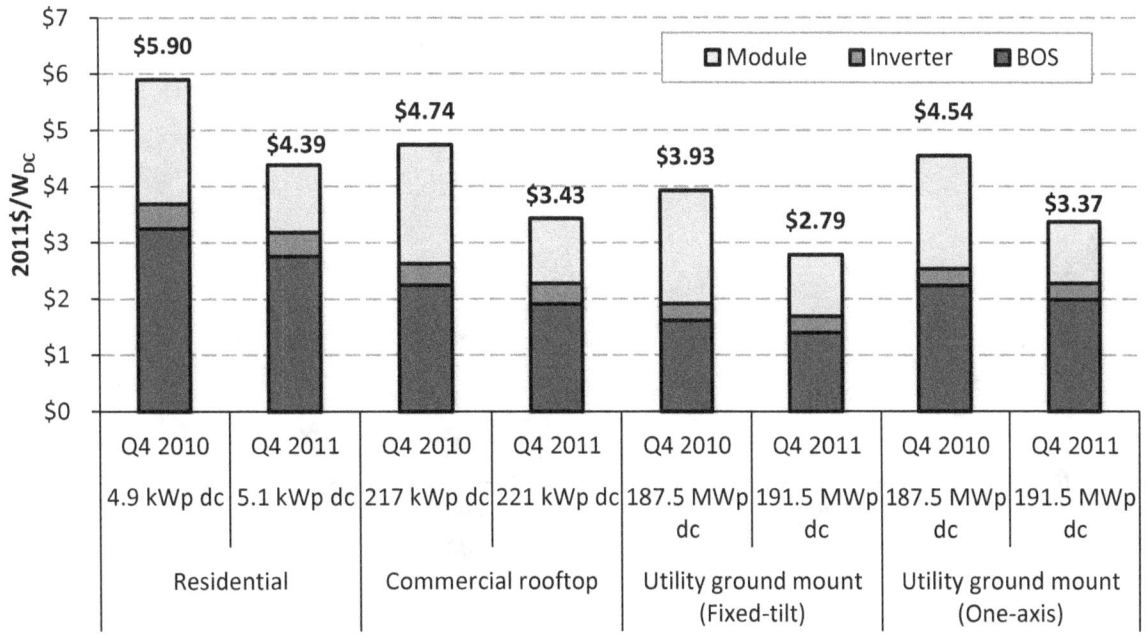

Figure 9. Bottom-up modeled installed PV system prices by sector, Q4 2010 and Q4 2011

Note: Standard crystalline silicon modules (14.5% efficiency in Q4 2010 and 14.9% in Q4 2011). The increase in module efficiency is the cause for increased system size. Modeled system sizes in the residential and commercial rooftop sectors were chosen based on typical system sizes, then adjusted for optimal inverter configuration. System sizing for utility-scale benchmarks were chosen for comparison purposes against pricing reported from DOE's Energy Information Administration (2010).

System size has a significant and beneficial impact on rooftop and ground-mount system prices. Large PV systems not only better amortize fixed project overhead expenses—they also improve installer efficiencies and drive more efficient supply chain strategies. Figure 10 summarizes the modeled price benefits of increased system size across market segments. There are significant economies-of-scale within and across market segments, with diminishing returns as system size increases within each market segment.[19]

The efficiency of modules also affects the total price of a system. Across most PV technologies, the efficiency of commercially available PV modules varies from about 10% (for tandem microcrystalline-amorphous silicon) to 20% (for super monocrystalline silicon[20]). By increasing the power/efficiency of each module installed, the area-related costs of a system may be reduced. For relatively mature PV technologies like single-junction crystalline silicon, however, which are approaching a practical module efficiency limit from a manufacturing perspective, the value of additional efficiency gains is low relative to the value of improving the performance of lower efficiency thin-film modules. For example, improving the efficiency of modules used in a typical residential system (i.e., modeled as 4.9-kW roof mounted system in Q4 2010) from 10% to 11% provides $0.29/$W_{DC}$ of system-level cost savings, while improving the efficiency of modules used in the same system from 19% to 20% provides cost reductions of only $0.08/$W_{DC}$ (Goodrich et al. 2012).

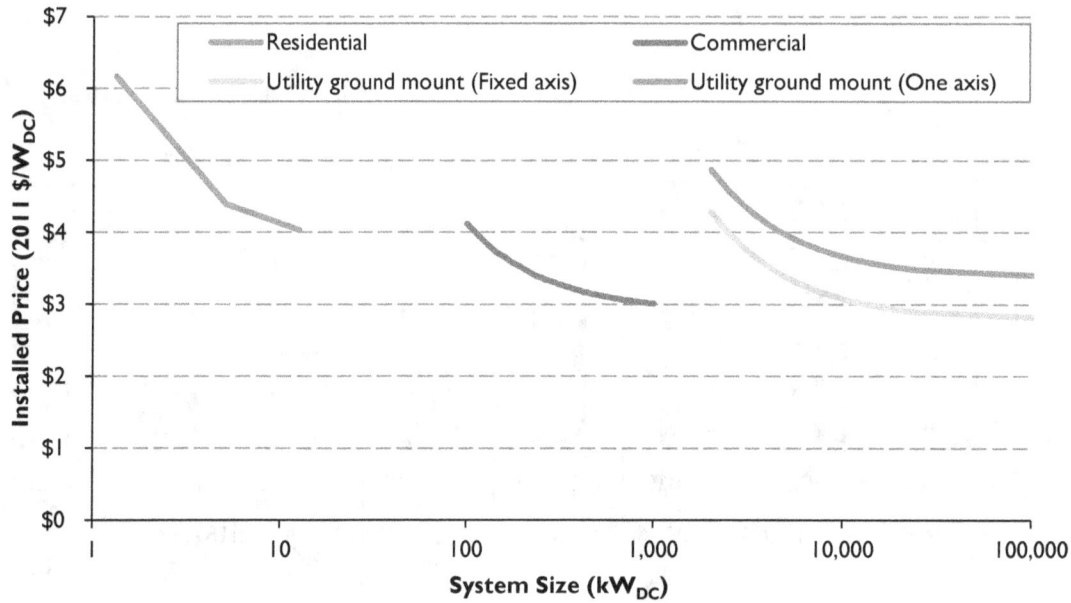

Figure 10. Economy-of-scale benefits: residential and commercial rooftop, ground-mount utility-scale PV, Q4 2011

4 Comparison Between Reported and Bottom-up Price Estimates

In theory, reported PV system prices (Section 2) should be similar to modeled bottom-up system prices (Section 3) for a given period. However, in practice, a number of factors can produce differences. Market factors, such as changes in incentive programs or price reporting methods, may alter reported system prices regardless of underlying component costs. Time lags might also affect reported prices; a project installed in a given year may reflect costs during that year or costs up to two years before, depending on the timing and contractual specifics of equipment sales and length of construction. Finally, the composition of the dataset of reported system prices—from geographic, technological, and average system size perspectives, as well as how they are permanently financed—can change each year.

In contrast, the bottom-up price benchmarks can keep fundamental system characteristics constant to track underlying cost changes consistently over time. At the same time, bottom-up benchmarks must rely, to some degree, on analyst judgment and simplifying assumptions, so they can diverge from actual underlying price movements if needed. Regardless of these potential differences, the reported price and bottom-up analyses presented in the previous sections produce reasonably similar PV price estimates.

Figure 11 compares 2011 reported PV system prices with bottom-up price benchmarks for Q4 2010. System prices from the reported price dataset represent the median price of residential and commercial systems and the capacity-weighted average price for utility-scale systems, and the error bars represent the $20^{th}/80^{th}$ percentiles of reported system prices for each market segment.

The bottom-up system price benchmarks are mean prices derived from an uncertainty analysis (using a Monte Carlo simulation) of published component data and installer-reported information, and the error bars represent one standard deviation above and below the mean (see Appendix A of Goodrich et al. [2012]). The Q4 2010 bottom-up prices are compared with reported price data for systems installed in 2011 because the benchmarks represent an installer's bid for a given system, which typically precedes the date of installation by several months or more; thus PV systems that are bid in Q4 2010 would most likely be placed in service in 2011.

The system categories and system sizes from the analysis of the reported price dataset and the bottom-up price benchmarks are not identical. Under the "residential" category in Figure 11, the median price of reported systems is calculated from pricing data for commercial and residential systems of 10 kW or smaller (with a median size of 5.0 kW), whereas the bottom-up benchmark price represents a modeled 4.9-kW residential system. Under the "commercial" category, the median reported price is calculated from pricing data for commercial systems larger than 100 kW (with a median size of 281 kW), whereas the bottom-up benchmark price represents a modeled 217-kW commercial system. Under the "utility-scale" category, the capacity-weighted average reported price is calculated from pricing data for ground-mounted systems 2 MW or larger (with a capacity-weighted average size of 18.3 MW), whereas the bottom-up benchmark price represents a modeled 187.5-MW ground-mounted fixed-tilt system. These categories were chosen because they are the most comparable between the analysis of reported system prices and bottom-up price benchmarks, but their lack of equivalence is another source of variability in the system price estimates.

With these assumptions and categorizations, there is significant overlap between the two analyses' price ranges, and the bottom-up price benchmarks fall well within the 20th/80th percentile ranges for each market sector of the reported price dataset (Figure 11). The similar results from the two analyses, which employ substantially different methodologies, support the validity of both sets of results and provide a consistent perspective on system pricing.

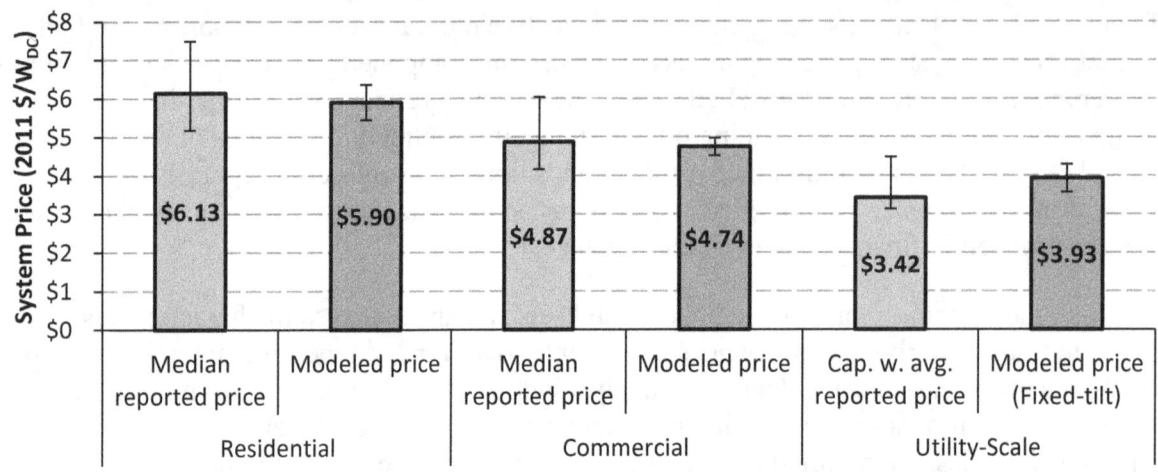

Figure 11. 2011 reported median (residential/commercial) and capacity-weighted average (utility-scale) prices vs. Q4 2010 bottom-up benchmark prices

Note: Error bars for the modeled price data represent one standard deviation above or below mean. Error bars for the median price data represent 20th/80th percentile of datasets. The median reported price for the residential market is representative of reported systems less than or equal to 10 kW in size; the median size of these systems is 5.0 kW. The bottom-up benchmark of residential systems models a 4.9-kW system. The median reported price for the commercial market is representative of reported systems greater than 100 kW in size; the median size of these systems is 281 kW. The bottom-up benchmark of commercial systems models a 217-kW rooftop system. The capacity-weighted average reported price for the utility-scale market is representative of reported systems greater than 2 MW in size; the capacity-weighted average size of these systems is 18.3 MW. The bottom-up benchmark of fixed-tilt utility-scale systems models a 187.5-MW ground-mounted system.

5 Near-Future Price Trends

Text Box 1 showed that continued reductions in reported PV prices are anticipated in 2012, while Section 3 demonstrated steep price reductions for Q4 2011 in comparison to Q4 2010. Additionally, as discussed in Text Box 2, U.S. system prices continue to be higher than prices in other, more mature global markets, such as Germany. This difference suggests that, as the U.S. market continues to grow in annual and cumulative capacity, substantially lower system prices should be possible (notwithstanding structural differences between the U.S. and German markets).

Text Box 2. Comparison of German and U.S. PV System Prices

Figure 12 compares the median price of German PV systems *quoted* in 2011 to the median price of U.S. systems *installed* in 2011. The price of the German systems is well below the price of similarly sized U.S. systems. Although not perfectly comparable (e.g., the German data are based on price quotes for prospective systems, while the U.S. data are based on systems installed), these data suggest that significant near-term cost reductions are possible within the United States. Given that hardware costs are largely equivalent across countries, much of the gap between PV prices in the United States and Germany can be attributed to differences in "soft costs" (Seel et al. 2012).

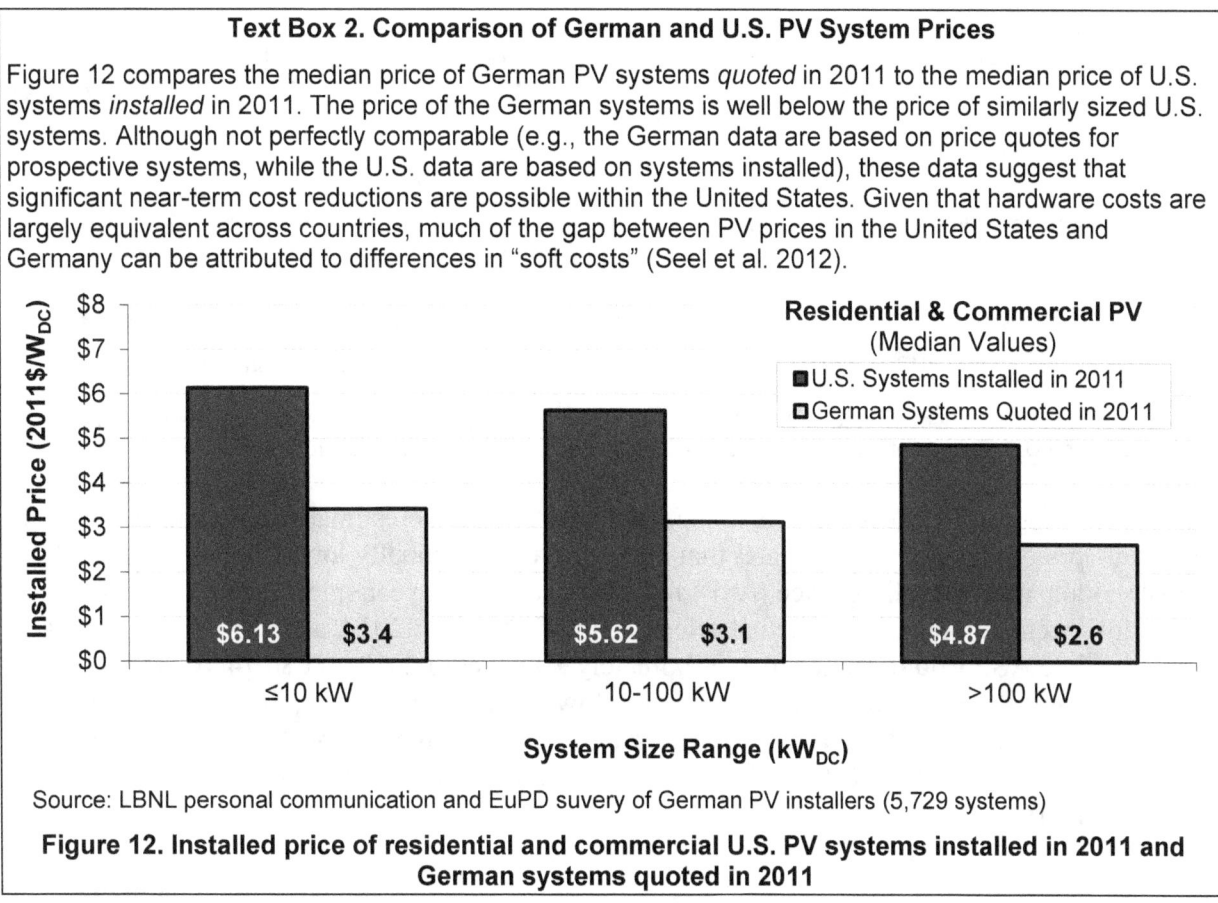

Source: LBNL personal communication and EuPD suvery of German PV installers (5,729 systems)

Figure 12. Installed price of residential and commercial U.S. PV systems installed in 2011 and German systems quoted in 2011

As shown in Figure 13, most analysts also project that PV system price trends will maintain their downward trajectory in the near term. Owing to the global scope of most solar companies, analysts often project system prices across sectors and countries. Figure 13 depicts the range in analyst projections for the average price of distributed and utility-scale systems through 2013. The 11 projections (six for utility-scale PV, five for distributed PV) vary in their focus on specific companies, countries, and sectors. The lower end of the distributed PV range mostly comprises projections for countries with low pricing environments, whereas the upper end of the range comprises projections for more expensive markets. These ranges only depict the variety in average price projections, not the range of price projections for specific projects.

As Figure 13 shows, the range of price projections is trending downward in the near term. Projected declines in PV hardware costs contribute to the projected decline in system prices. Analysts project an oversupply of PV components (polysilicon, wafers, cells, modules, and inverters) relative to projected global demand, particularly from manufacturers in low cost regions that have scaled rapidly and integrated vertically.

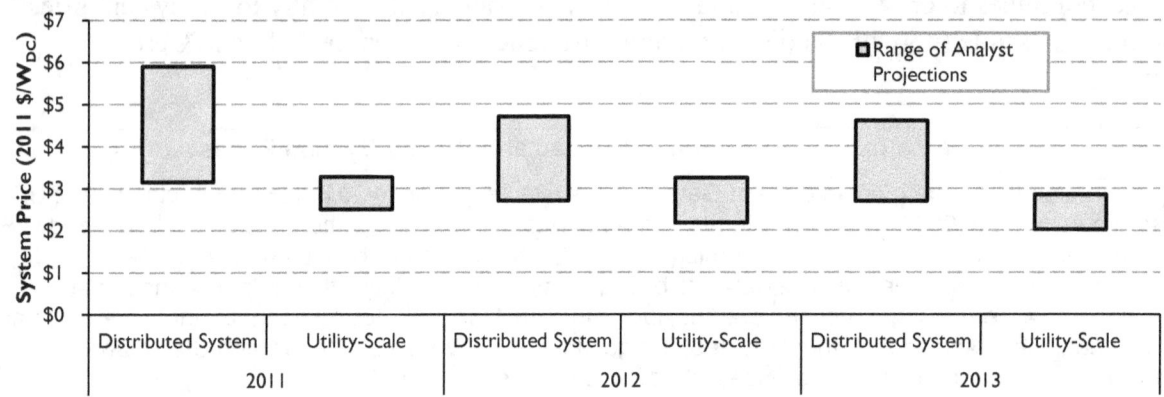

Figure 13. Analyst estimates (2011) and projections (2012–2013) of global average system price

Sources: Bloomberg (2012); Citigroup (6/7/12); Deutsche Bank (2/29/12 & 3/8/12); Photon Consulting (2012)

Note: Nominal dollars were converted to 2011$ using the "Monthly Consumer Price Index for All Urban Consumers," published by the U.S. Bureau of Labor Statistics (2012) and the U.S. Energy Information Administration (2012)

As shown in Figure 14, most analysts in recent history have underestimated the rapid reductions in module prices. This figure illustrates that analysts have continually lowered their estimated global module average selling price (ASP) for future years each year since 2008, but most projections were still higher than actual prices. In the first half of 2012, analysts estimated that global module ASP would decline to approximately $0.82/W in 2012 and $0.74/W in 2013. Some companies are currently selling modules below this level, indicating that even further price reductions beyond these recent analyst projects are plausible. Though not shown here, analysts project inverter and BOS costs to decline over this period as well, placing further pressure on total system prices.

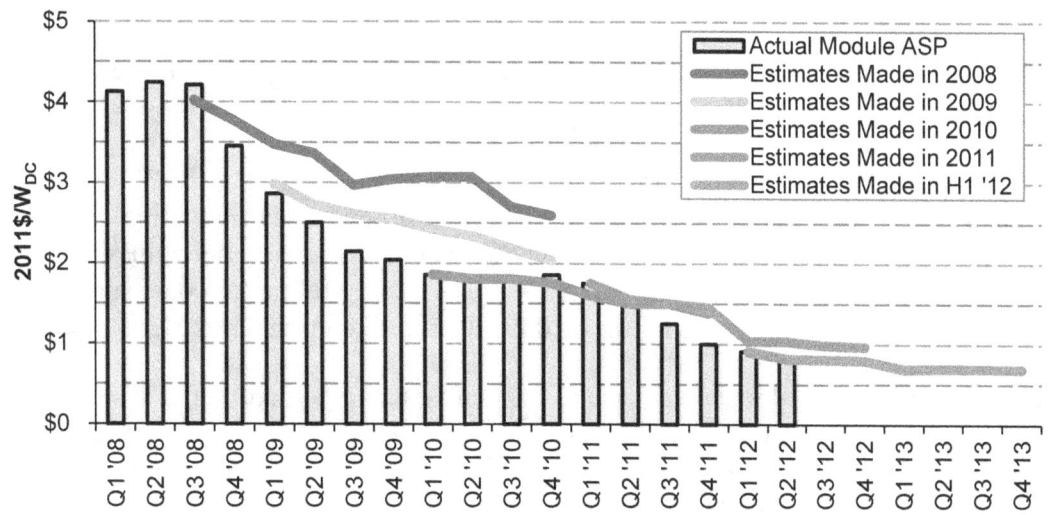

Figure 14. Actual module average selling price reduction vs. average analyst expectations

Sources: Barclays (05/01/09, 11/15/10, & 04/11/11); Citigroup (05/01/12); Deutsche Bank (05/27/08, 01/21/09, 05/06/10, & 01/05/11); Goldman Sachs (10/17/11, 02/29/12, & 06/26/12); Lazard (11/04/08, & 04/02/09); Stifel Nicolaus (07/15/11, 01/25/12, & 04/20/12); Thomas Weisel (10/06/09, & 04/08/10); UBS (08/22/10, 03/08/11, and 10/10/11)

Note: Nominal dollars were converted to 2011$ using the "Monthly Consumer Price Index for All Urban Consumers," published by the U.S. Bureau of Labor Statistics (2012) and the U.S. Energy Information Administration (2012).

6 Conclusion

This summary report provides an overview of historical, recent, and projected near-term PV pricing trends in the United States—focusing on the installed price of PV systems.

Reported price data from an extensive sample of more than 150,000 installed PV systems show substantial system price reductions over time, and variability in prices depending on system size, configuration, and location. Installed prices of U.S. residential and commercial PV systems declined 5%–7% per year, on average, during 1998–2011, and preliminary data suggest that even steeper price reductions, as witnessed during 2009–2011, will continue in 2012.

In 2011, the median reported installed price of residential and commercial PV systems was $6.13/W for systems of 10 kW or smaller, $5.62/W for systems of 10–100 kW, and $4.87/W for systems larger than 100 kW. The capacity-weighted average reported installed price of utility-scale PV systems (ground-mounted systems at least 2 MW in size) declined from $6.21/W during 2004–2008 to $3.42/W in 2011. The drop in installed system prices has resulted from module and non-module cost reductions, but module costs have declined more quickly, thus heightening the PV industry's recent emphasis on reducing non-module costs.

The complementary bottom-up modeling analysis—which aims to minimize some of the potential market distortions associated with the reported price analysis—indicates 2011 installed prices (based on Q4 2010 benchmarks) of $5.90/W for 4.9-kW residential systems, $4.74/W for 217-kW commercial rooftop systems, $3.93/W for 187.5-MW fixed-tilt utility-scale systems, and $4.54/W for 187.5-MW one-axis-tracking utility-scale systems.

For each system type, BOS constitutes the largest cost component, followed by module costs and inverter costs. Increasing system size and improving module efficiency both reduce the estimated per-watt system price, although there are points at which these improvements provide diminishing returns. The data sources, assumptions, and methods differ substantially between the bottom-up analysis and the reported price analysis; however, the results are similar, which supports the validity of both analyses and provides a consistent perspective on system pricing.

The bottom-up analysis further indicates that 2012 installed system prices (based on Q4 2011 benchmarks) will likely continue to decline. The Q4 2011 benchmarks are $4.39/W for 5.1-kW residential systems, $3.43/W for 221-kW commercial rooftop systems, $2.79/W for 191.5-MW fixed-tilt utility-scale systems, and $3.37/W for 191.5-MW one-axis-tracking utility-scale systems.

Most analysts also project that PV price trends will maintain their downward trajectory in the near term as PV hardware costs continue to decline. Analysts estimate that the global module average selling price will decline from $1.37/W in 2011 to approximately $0.74/W by 2013 and that inverter prices will also decline over this period (Mints 2012). Germany's current PV price advantage suggests that substantial BOS cost reductions are possible for U.S. systems as well.

References

Ardani, K.; Barbose, G.; Margolis, R.; Wiser, R.; Feldman, D.; Ong, S. (2012). *Benchmarking Non-Hardware Balance-of-System (Soft) Costs for U.S. Photovoltaic Systems Using a Bottom-Up Approach and Installer Survey.* Golden, CO: National Renewable Energy Laboratory. Berkeley, CA: Lawrence Berkeley National Laboratory.

Barbose, G.; Darghouth, N.; Wiser, R. (2012). *Tracking the Sun V: An Historical Summary of the Installed Price of Photovoltaics in the United States from 1998 to 2011.* Berkeley, CA: Lawrence Berkeley National Laboratory.

Barclays Capital. U.S. Clean Technology: Cleantech Insights V27. Shah, V. et al. Apr. 11, 2011.

Barclays Capital. U.S. Clean Technology: German Solar IRRs, Replacement Values. Shah, V. et al. Nov. 15, 2010.

Barclays Capital. Solar Energy Handbook. Shah, V. May 1, 2009.

Bloomberg New Energy Finance. PV Market Outlook, Q1 2012 (Bloomberg New Energy Finance, 2012).

Bureau of Labor Statistics. (2012). *Consumer Price Index - All Urban Consumers.* http://data.bls.gov/cgi-bin/surveymost. Accessed Aug. 22, 2012.

Citigroup Global Markets. Global Renewable Beat: Daily. Arcuri, T. et al. Jun. 7, 2012.

Citigroup Global Markets. Signs of a Near-Term Bottom. Arcuri, T. May 1, 2012.

Deutsche Bank Securities Inc. Solar Photovoltaic Industry: 2011 Outlook. Kim, P. et al. Jan. 5, 2011.

Deutsche Bank Securities Inc. Solar Photovoltaic Industry: Looking through the storm. O'Rourke, S. et al. Jan. 21, 2009.

Deutsche Bank Securities Inc. Solar Photovoltaic Industry: Solar PV industry outlook and economics. O'Rourke, S. et al. May 27, 2008.

Deutsche Bank Securities Inc. Solar Photovoltaics: Financing a strategic industry in the United States. O'Rourke, S. et al. May 6, 2010.

Deutsche Bank Securities Inc. First Solar Inc.: Warranty Charges Impact Q4; Guide Better Than Feared. Shah, V. et al. Feb. 20, 2012).

Deutsche Bank Securities Inc. Suntech Power Holdings: Balance Sheet, Margins Could Remain Near Term Overhang. Shah, V. et al. Mar. 8, 2012).

Goldman Sachs Global Investment Research. Stay cautious on the fading rally. Benson, S. et al. Feb. 29, 2012.

Goldman Sachs Global Investment Research. Traversing Clean Energy's Unpaved Path; Q3 11 Outlook. Wienkes, M. et al. Oct. 17, 2011.

Goldman Sachs Global Investment Research. Vicious circle delays solar supply chain rationalization. Song, A. et al. Jun. 26, 2012.

Goodrich, A.; James, T.; Woodhouse, M. (2012). *Residential, Commercial, and Utility-Scale Photovoltaic (PV) System Prices in the United States: Current Drivers and Cost-Reduction Opportunities.* NREL/TP-6A20-53347. Golden, CO: National Renewable Energy Laboratory. http://www.nrel.gov/docs/fy12osti/53347.pdf.

Lazard Capital Markets. Alternative Energy & Infrastructure: a framework for assessing solar stocks in turbulent times. Shrestha, S. et al. Apr. 2, 2009.

Lazard Capital Markets. Alternative Energy & Infrastructure: Solar sector. Shrestha, S. et al. Nov. 4, 2008.

Mints, P. (2011). *Analysis of Worldwide Markets for Solar Products and Five-Year Application Forecast 2010/2011.* Report # NPS-Global6. Palo Alto, CA: Navigant Consulting Photovoltaic Service Program.

Mints, P. (2012). *Photovoltaic Manufacturer Shipments, Capacity & Competitive Analysis 2011/2012.* Report # NPS-Supply7. Palo Alto, CA: Navigant Consulting Photovoltaic Service Program.

Photon Consulting. *Solar Annual 2012: The Next Wave.* Mayank, A. et al. 2012.

Seel, J.; Barbose, G.; Wiser, R. (2012). "Why Are Residential PV Prices in Germany So Much Lower Than in the United States? A Scoping Analysis." Berkeley, CA: Lawrence Berkeley National Laboratory.

SEIA and GTM Research. (March 2012). "U.S. Solar Market Insight Report: Q4 2011 & 2011 Year-In-Review."

SEIA and GTM Research. (September 2012). "U.S. Solar Market Insight Report: Q2 2012."

Stifel, Nicolaus & Company, Inc. Stifel Nicolaus Green Sheet: Vol. 5, No. 3. Osborne, J. et al. Jul. 15, 2011.

Stifel, Nicolaus & Company, Inc. Stifel Nicolaus Green Sheet: Vol. 6, No. 1. Osborne, J. et al. Jan. 25, 2012.

Stifel, Nicolaus & Company, Inc. Stifel Nicolaus Green Sheet: Vol. 6, No. 2. Osborne, J. et al. Apr. 20, 2012.

Thomas Weisel Partners. TWP Green Sheet: Vol. 3, No. 4. Osborne, J. et al. Oct. 6, 2009.

Thomas Weisel Partners. TWP Green Sheet: Vol. 4, No. 2. Osborne, J. et al. Apr. 8, 2010.

UBS Investment Research. Global I/O: Solar Industry. Chin, S. et al. Aug. 22, 2010.

UBS Investment Research. Global I/O: Solar Industry. Chin, S. et al. Mar. 8, 2011.

UBS Investment Research. Global I/O: Solar Industry. Chin, S. et al. Oct. 10, 2011.

U.S. Energy Information Administration. (2012). *AEO2012 National Energy Modeling System.* http://www.eia.gov/oiaf/aeo/tablebrowser/aeo_query_server/?event=ehExcel.getFile&study=AEO2012&region=0-0&cases=ref2012-d020112c&table=18-AEO2012&yearFilter=0. Accessed Aug. 22, 2012.

U.S. Energy Information Administration. (2010). *Updated Capital Cost Estimates for Electricity Generation Plants.* November 2010. http://www.eia.gov/oiaf/beck_plantcosts/pdf/updatedplantcosts.pdf. Accessed Oct. 16, 2012.

---

[1] All prices are reported in real 2011 dollars per watt of DC electricity generated, and all system sizes are reported in W, kW, or MW of DC electricity generated under standard test conditions, unless otherwise noted.

[2] The overnight capital cost is the capital cost of a project if it could be constructed overnight at the time of the estimate. For this analysis, financing costs are not included, but interest costs during construction are included.

[3] U.S. installations (2006-2009) and global installations (2006-2010): Mints (2011). Global installations (2011): Mints (2012). U.S. installations (2010-2011): SEIA & GTM (March 2012).

[4] In this report, "commercial" PV includes ground- and roof-mounted systems installed at public-sector, non-profit, and for-profit customer sites, regardless of whether electricity is delivered to the customer or utility side of the electrical meter. "Utility-scale" PV refers to ground-mounted systems larger than 2 MW.

[5] LBNL and NREL collect and compile data from PV incentive programs to support LBNL's annual *Tracking the Sun* report series and NREL's *OpenPV* online data-visualization tool (https://openpv.nrel.gov).

[6] Colorado is not represented because its primary PV incentive program administrator was unwilling to contribute data. Hawaii is not represented because its primary incentive program does not collect system-level installed price data. All other major PV incentive programs and markets are well represented in the final data sample.

[7] For utility-scale and large commercial PV project data sourced from the Section 1603 Grant Program database, the installed price is estimated by assuming that the grant is equal to 30% of the installed price.

[8] The issue of appraised value reporting is specific to TPO residential and commercial systems installed by integrated companies that provide the installation service and the customer financing. In these cases, the price reported to incentive program administrators is typically based on the appraised value of a larger bundle of systems, and those appraised values historically have been considerably higher than the reported price for host-customer-owned systems. For example, among systems of 10 kW or less installed in 2011, systems installed by integrated third-party-financing providers had a median price of $7.98/W, compared with $6.04/W for host-customer-owned systems. In contrast, the price reported to incentive program managers for TPO systems financed by non-integrated providers is typically the actual sales price for the transaction between the customer-finance provider and the contractor who installed the system. These systems were not screened from the data sample because the reported prices were deemed to be roughly--though not perfectly--comparable to the purchase price for host-customer-owned systems.

[9] The screening approach began by identifying clusters of residential and commercial systems with identical nominal prices. Systems within these price clusters were then screened out based on available information about installer name and TPO status. If the system was known to be either host-customer owned or installed by a company that is not an integrated TPO provider, then it was retained in the data sample; otherwise, the system was removed. In addition, all known TPO systems installed by integrated providers, regardless of whether they reside within a price cluster, were removed from the data sample. As a result of this screening process, roughly 5% of all residential and commercial systems and 12% of 2011 systems were removed from the initial data sample. See Barbose et al. (2012) for further methodological details.

[10] In terms of capacity, the sample is somewhat less skewed toward California, which accounts for 50% of all residential and commercial capacity in the sample and 41% of the 2011 residential and commercial capacity additions.

[11] The gap between the final, cleaned data sample and the total U.S. grid-connected PV market consists of PV systems that were dropped from the data sample, residential and commercial PV systems not funded by any of the PV incentive programs that contributed data to the analysis, and utility-sector PV systems for which reliable cost data could not be obtained.

[12] The imperfect correlation between movements in global average module prices and installed system prices may reflect any number of underlying dynamics, including the lag between the time of module sale by the manufacturer and the time of system installation, or value-based pricing associated with a lack of competitive pressure in particular markets and/or rich incentives.

[13] NREL and LBNL benchmarked the non-hardware, business process costs of U.S. PV systems based on a survey of PV installers; see Ardani et al. (2012).

[14] The high median price and wide percentile bands for Texans are driven, in large part, by a single installer with a large number of relatively small (just over 10 kW) high priced, host-customer-owned systems.

[15] This rough upper-bound on sales tax costs is calculated based on a total sales tax rate of 9% (the sum of state and local sales taxes in some portions of California) and an installed price of $6.40/W (the median for California systems ≤10 kW), assuming that 70% of the total system price is subject to sales taxes (as determined from project-level data identifying underlying sales tax costs).

[16] SEIA and GTM (March 2012) reported 1.1 GW of utility-scale PV installed in the United States as of the end of 2011, though the definition of utility-scale used within that analysis is not exactly comparable to the definition used within the present report.

[17] A capacity-weighted average is used in this case rather than a median value (as was used for residential and commercial systems), owing to the large number of relatively small systems (2–5 MW) within the utility-scale PV project data sample but considering the arguably greater relevance of larger utility-scale projects.

[18] Because the NREL bottom-up methodology is structured as the system price an installer would offer for a system, the prices do not include the cost of financing after construction, which may be incorporated into the reported prices of actual PV systems. This financing cost can be significant for large PV installations, particularly for utility-scale systems. For a full description of NREL's bottom-up methodology, see Goodrich et al. (2012).

[19] There is also a possibility for diseconomies of scale beyond a certain size point for utility projects due to longer project development and construction timelines and possible additional costs of finding and using such a large amount of contiguous space. However, because most of these large PV systems (larger than 100 MW) have not yet come online and/or there are limited data for this market, it is not yet known at what point diseconomies of scale are achieved, if at all.

[20] Super monocrystalline PV modules are currently the most efficient single-junction crystalline silicon technology.

www.ingramcontent.com/pod-product-compliance
Lightning Source LLC
Chambersburg PA
CBHW082035190526
45165CB00020B/3283